FROM THE CROSS

FROM THE CROSS

Earl R. Jefferson, D.Min.

VANTAGE PRESS
New York

Cover design by Polly McQuillen

Published by Vantage Press, Inc.
419 Park Ave. South, New York, NY 10016

Manufactured in the United States of America
ISBN: 0-533-15261-5

Library of Congress Catalog Card No.: 2005904807

0 9 8 7 6 5 4 3 2 1

Contents

Foreword

In the midst of a world clamoring for knowledge and help in the area of sermon building and preaching, Dr. Earl R. Jefferson has once again stepped up to the plate and hit a home run. This publication joins those that have flowed from his prolific pen, providing tools and inspiration to those who embrace a passion for ministry and Christian education. Uniquely crafted and skillfully executed, this volume provides useful help that ushers the reader toward excellence in the study of the view from the cross.

It is an easy read, well-researched and written with a view toward undergirding the preaching endeavor, benefiting both the student and teacher alike. The simplistic style coupled with a wellspring of valuable information unite in a fountain of knowledge that whets the appetite and cultivates a craving for empowered and impassioned preaching. In this quest, Dr. Jefferson is most successful. Those who read the sermons in this publication and make use of its rich nuggets of knowledge will enhance their preaching skill level and come away better equipped for a strengthened journey in Christian living.

I am pleased to salute Dr. Earl R. Jefferson for his continuing contribution, which gives wings to the message from the cross. He is to be both congratulated and thanked for this outstanding contribution.

Bishop Richard Franklin Norris
116th Bishop of the African Methodist Episcopal Church
Presiding Prelate of the First Episcopal District

Preface

From the Cross is a compilation of sermon thoughts and ideas which were put to paper in response to the many requests, by lay people, for a book of meaningful and understandable devotional readings for the Easter season. Several young ministers have also asked for a tool that might help them with sermon preparation for the season.

"The Seven Last Words," it seemed, would be a most appropriate centerpiece for such a rendering.

My hope and my prayer is that it is brief enough to be picked up, clear enough to be read and understood, helpful enough to be used and shared, and compelling enough to make the reader want more.

Acknowledgments

Special thanks are extended to my wife, Betty, who read and re-read every draft, to my sons, Earl, Bruce, and Michael, and to my many ministerial colleagues and friends in Christian education who continue to prod, encourage, inspire, and ask questions.

Introduction

"A Man on a Mission"

Who Is He?

He entered as a king.
He was lauded by the crowd.
He asserted *His* authority.
He influenced the nation.
He became hated;
His perfect life condemned sinful men.
He watched, as the evil forces gained momentum.
He prepared for what God had ordained.
He prayed.
He spoke as no other had ever spoken.
While we were yet sinners, *He* died for us.
He returned to *His Father* in victory.
He arose from the dead.
He lives!

Amen

FROM THE CROSS

Forethought

"Rejoice greatly, O daughter of Zion; shout, O daughter of Jerusalem: behold, thy King cometh unto thee; he is just, and having salvation; lowly, and riding upon an ass, and upon a colt the foal of an ass."

—Zechariah 9:9 (KJV)

"And a very great multitude spread their garments in the way; others cut down branches from the trees, and strewed them in the way. And the multitudes that went before, and that followed, cried, saying, Hosanna to the son of David: Blessed is he that cometh in the name of the Lord; Hosanna in the highest. And when he was come to Jerusalem, all the city was moved, saying Who is this? And the multitude said, This is Jesus the prophet of Nazareth of Galilee."

—Matthew 21:8–11 (KJV)

"And they come to Jerusalem: and Jesus went into the temple, and began to cast out them that sold and bought in the temple, and overthrew the tables of the money changers, and the seats of them that sold doves; And would not suffer that any man should carry any vessel through the temple. And he taught, saying unto them, Is it not written, My house shall be called of all nations the house of prayer? but ye have made it a den of thieves."

—Mark 11:15–17 (KJV)

As Jesus neared the end of His third year of ministry, the time came due for the annual feast of the Passover. More than a million people had gathered in Jerusalem for this very special occasion. They had come, not only from every part of Palestine, but by land

and by sea. They had come from all of the countries where the seed of Abraham had been dispersed.

Some came with solemn thoughts and deep spiritual and religious joy. Some came for reunion with relatives and long-lost friends. Some came just to be in the number while others, of a baser sort, came to sell their goods, hoping to vastly advance their personal enterprises. Yes, this year, the minds of all were filled with unusual excitement; everybody came looking for something more remarkable than they had ever seen. They came hoping to see Jesus at the feast, and had all kinds of strange ideas about what might happen in connection with Him.

The name of Jesus had been noised around everywhere; everybody had heard about Him. Among the pilgrims on the highways, among the Jewish groups on ships from Asia Minor—everybody was talking about Jesus. Who was He? Who was this unusual man, Jesus?

His disciples, of course, were also there, hoping above hope that He would finally let the people know who He really was; that He would cast aside the guise of humility which had hidden His glory and would, in some unquestionable way, demonstrate His Messiahship.

There must have been at least a thousand people there from the southern part of the country, who had come with the same enthusiastic zeal as entertained in Galilee. And there were, of course, those who were not positively disposed to Jesus.

Tens of thousands of those who had heard about Him but had never seen Him came to see a miracle or to hear a profound word from the new prophet. Those in authority in Jerusalem were also there waiting for Him, but their agenda was very different. They wanted to trick Him. They wanted to discredit Him. They wanted to turn the people against Him. They hoped that the events of the day would turn things around in their favor, and that they would finally be able to stop Jesus in His tracks.

A vast crowd had been with Jesus during the last twenty miles of His journey; He had been the center of attraction. They had seen Him heal blind Bartimaeus at Jericho, and they were all excited about what. When they arrived at Bethany, the village was still ringing with talk about the resurrection of Lazarus. Everybody was excited.

As Jesus drew near Bethany at the Mount of Olives, He sent two of His disciples ahead of Him, saying: "Go into the city that we are about to enter and you will find a colt on which no man has ever sat. Loose the colt and bring it to me. And if any man asks why do you loose it, tell him that the Lord hath need of it."

As they were untying the colt, its owner asked: "Why are you untying the colt?"

The disciples answered: "The Lord hath need of it." Then they took the colt, led it to Jesus, spread their clothing on its back, and Jesus sat upon it.

As Jesus rode through the city, a vast assemblage of people gathered and cried out with joy, "Hosanna, hosanna (*save now, save now*), blessed be the name of the Lord."

The Gospel writer, Mark, had an unusual way of symbolically making stories such as this relevant even for today, in these challenging and ever changing times. The waving of *palms,* for instance, was not just a casual happening; it was a political action, like waving a flag. It was an indication to the people that Jesus was a person of great significance; one who had come to liberate their homeland from foreign rule. *The disciples* being sent out by Jesus in this particular situation clearly represent our pastors of today, who are commissioned by God to go out and seek the most tender of souls. Those whom they seek are to carry the message of Jesus. Jesus sent for *a colt* on which to ride—not a man-carried palanquin not a horse-drawn carriage, not a chariot—*a colt*. The colt can be likened to *an ordinary person*—not a king nor a queen, not an emperor nor a monarch—*an ordinary person* just like you or me. And the city—*the Ekklesia*—is, of course, *the church*. That is

3

to say, the pastors are to seek out the souls to carry the message of Jesus in the church.

It is the next morning and Jesus sets out on a short walk around the Mount of Olives. He is hungry. No doubt the crowds were so vast in Bethany that those around Him were not able to get food for Him. He sees a fig tree full of leaves, and seems disappointed that there are no figs on it. He curses the fig tree and moves on. (The cursing of the fig tree is obviously an indication of His disappointment with those who honor God with their mouths, but whose lives belie their words.)

When Jesus reaches the city, He goes into the temple and, to His dismay, He finds money changers, sellers of doves, and other business people (seizing an unauthorized opportunity to use the assemblage for personal gain and to take advantage) gainfully employed in plying their wares supposedly for religious purposes. He sees porters using the temple as a thoroughfare or a shortcut from one place to another. Without any warning, He turns over the tables of the money changers and the stools of the sellers, and He blocks the access way of those carrying goods through the temple courtyard. Then He states boldly, "It is written in the scripture that God said, 'My temple will be called a house of prayer for the people of all nations.' But you have made it a den of thieves."

By this bold action, Jesus wrecked the monopoly of the Sadducees and, from that point on, the chief priests and the teachers of the law began looking for ways to do away with Jesus.

Although many years have passed, the mode of operation of many "believers" does not seem to have changed: circumstances, conditions, and situations in our churches today are not too different from the way they were in the temple on that Monday morning in Jesus' day. Some people who attend church have solemn thoughts of deep spiritual and religious joy. Some attend for the purpose of reunion with family members and friends. Some just want to be in the number. There are others who are looking to see a miracle or are hoping to hear a word from a prophet. There are some who are just passing through because it is convenient. Some attend who are opportunistic exploiters who hope to gain financially by being in that environment. Others attend in order to let people know who they are and what they can do, having little or no regard for what God might want them to do. And yes, there are those who attend who feel that if they cannot have things their way, that Jesus needs to be eliminated from the situation.

But now, just like then, Jesus is not the least bit concerned about the prospect of disrupters being successful. Rather, during this Lenten season—this season of reflection and retrospection, this season of personal inventory and sacrifice, this season of repentance, this season of changing our hearts, our minds and our ways of doing things, this season of moving away from the un-Godly to the God-like, this season during which we live out the experience of the life, the trial, the crucifixion, the death, and the resurrection of Jesus the Christ—He has the Gospel writer, Mark, to remind us that Jesus is in the temple and that He is looking for people like you and me: people who will love Him, who will worship and praise Him, who will commit themselves to serve Him, and who will follow Him. He is looking for people like you and me, who will work toward bringing into being His Kingdom here on earth.

He is going to be blocking the access way of those who are just passing through. (We will not have to be concerned about that.) He is going to turn over the tables of the money changers and the stools of the other exploiters. (He will have that under control.) But He wants us to understand that the church is not to be a hideout for thieves, not a museum for displaying the saints, and not a shortcut or a special route to our personal destinations. He is not going to let people ply their wares nor perpetuate their "own thing" in God's house. (He is going to take care of those problematic situations.)

5

Jesus wants us to know, however, that the church *is* to be: a way station for the exploited, a lighthouse for the lost, a comfort center for the oppressed, and a hospital for the sin-sick soul. He tells us, also, not to become weary in what we are doing but, rather, to keep on trusting, praying, praising, loving, sharing, and doing God's will. No matter how bleak the situation may appear to us, He says: "Come unto me all ye that labor and are heavy laden and I will give you rest." There is no need to clean up, or get yourself ready, or check with your neighbor; if you are weary and heavy laden, "Come . . . and I will give you rest."

> "I pray for them: I pray not for the world, but for them which thou hast given me; for they are thine. And all mine are thine, and thine are mine; and I am glorified in them. And now I am no more in the world, but these are in the world, and I come to thee."
>
> —John 17:9–11 (KJV)

Before the Cross

His focus was clear:
He would maintain His relationship
with the remaining disciples and
His unity with the Father.
His focus was clear:
He would tell the disciples . . .
His focus was clear:
He would borrow a banquet hall and
sup with those who would continue . . .
His focus was clear:
He would set an example by washing their feet . . .
His focus was clear:
He had to let them know
that they would not be left alone;
that the Comforter would come.
His focus was clear:
He had to take the journey alone.
His focus was clear:
He would fall before His father
in humble submission.
His focus was clear:
Life could only come through death!
His focus was clear:
He would arise . . . !

One of the Nails—I Was There

I had always dreamed of myself as one of the nails which would go to support and hold together one of the great tables in the marketplace. I had imagined feeling my superior strength and power as I was driven through one freshly cut piece of wood into another, easily holding them together securely. I had often thought of the challenge that would be mine to hold up my end, when the table had piled high with goods, and I was certain that when the others had given in, I would still be holding fast. I had looked forward to seeing all the people of power, position, and station in life who would come through the marketplace, and I anticipated the joy and pride that I would experience when they stopped in front of me.

One day, however, something strange happened. The box in which I had been anxiously waiting fell to the ground and, although the other nails around me were swept together and, I guess, scooped up and returned to the box, I was pushed aside and left. I laid there for about five days. I had no idea where I was, but I do know that I was kicked, stepped on, pushed aside, and rained on before I was finally picked up.

I was put in a dirty bag with two other nails, both of which were smaller, cleaner, and newer than I, but neither of which had the girth, the strength, or the power with which I had been endowed. I felt superior again; I began, again, to feel that I was necessary. I lay there, with the others, attempting to prepare myself physically and emotionally for some great task that I was sure awaited me. I tried to rest.

I must have dozed off but was awakened by the shouts and

jeers of many people around me. I could not figure out what was going on but, amidst it all, a big, dirty hand was thrust into the bag and roughly pulled out, dropping two of us.

We fell at the feet of a man who, although seemingly young, appeared extremely worn. He was lying on his back with his arms stretched out as if he were completely exhausted. We didn't know who he was but, for some unknown reason, it appeared as though the people were laughing at him and mocking him; calling him some kind of a king. It seemed very strange, though, to see a king in such disarray.

I watched the man who had taken me from the bag, with hammer in hand, move toward the left hand of the king. With apparently nothing needing to be nailed in front of him, I saw him raise the hammer and strike a blow, then another and another.

Hearing the voice of the king, I felt pain. A soldier picked up the other nail, which lay beside me, and moved toward the other side. I tried to let my mind become consumed by the noise around me but I could not block out the cries of anguish and pain as the soldier administered several more dreadful blows.

My countenance dropped and my spirit left as I anticipated my fate. The soldier came and got me and, with no ado, placed me on the foot of the agonizing king who lay on the cross. With one crashing blow my spear-like end thrashed through the skin, past bone, through skin and skin, past bone, and through skin again. A second blow sent me into a piece of roughly hewn oak; a third lodged me securely.

I was repulsed by the realization of what I had been chosen to do. A feeling of revulsion came over me as I felt the blood moving around my stem and the skin of his feet, in sucking pulsation, clinging fast.

As the heavy piece of oak was arighted, I could feel the full weight of this man who seemed so small, yet who must have been carrying the weight of many on his shoulders. The weight which he carried was more than I could bear and I lapsed into unconsciousness, feeling acutely the fullness of this man, whose body and life had touched me.

The Cross Became His Throne

"Now is the
judgment
of this world:
now shall the prince of this
world be cast out. And I, if
I be lifted
up from the
earth, will
draw all men
unto me."

—John 12:31, 32 (KJV)

The First Word from the Cross

"Forgiveness"

"And when they were come to the place, which is called Calvary, there they crucified him, and the malefactors, one on the right hand, and other on the left. Then said Jesus, **Father, forgive them; for they know not what they do.** And they parted his raiment, and cast lots."

—Luke 23:33, 34 (KJV)

"For God so loved the world, that he gave his only begotten Son, that whosoever believeth in him should not perish, but have everlasting life. For God sent not his Son into the world to condemn the world; but that the world through him might be saved."

—John 3:16, 17 (KJV)

In reading these words, we know that Jesus came here on a great mission. He came and set out to accomplish a magnanimous task. He came into a world that was wrought with discomfort and pain, injustice and cruelty, oppression—even death. He came into a world of evil, misguided, misdirected, confused people; a world of sin. But He came, not to condemn the world—not to make fun of it, not to hurt it, not to burden it, not to put it down—but that the world through Him might be saved.

He healed the sick (made the blind to see, made the deaf to hear, made the lame to walk, made the leper whole), He raised the dead, He preached good news to the poor—He did all kinds of

11

things to aid people in gaining a more abundant life, yet they crucified Him. They crucified Him!

Despite this thanks of dubious repute, He still had a mind to pray, and not for Himself, but for those whom we feel should have been condemned: those who were against Him, those who had condemned Him, those who would crucify Him. "*Father forgive them; for they know not what they do.*"

In this instance, Jesus was practicing what He had so often preached. ("Ye have heard that it hath been said, Thou shalt love thy neighbor, and hate thine enemy. But I say unto you, Love your enemies, . . . pray for them which despitefully use you." And again, he admonished His followers to forgive, not once, but "seventy times seven"—that is, without limit. Here He was asking His Father to forgive without limit.)

You see, Jesus knew that **prayer changes people** and that *people change things;* He knew, too, that some changes needed to take place.

Prayer was not new to Jesus; in fact, it had become such a habit with Him that even under these most unusual circumstances—the insensitivity, the cruelty, the humiliation, the anguish, the pain—He just did what He was used to doing. Time and time again we read that He went to a solitary place to pray. We can only speculate about the nature and the content of His prayers, but the commentaries let us know that He certainly did not pray that all discomfort and pain would disappear or that all injustice and cruelty would pass away. We can be sure that He did not pray for an immediate eradication of hunger and disease, or that there would be no more death, or that His Father's Kingdom would come at that very moment. Rather, realizing that **prayer changes people** and that **people change things,** I would venture to think that Jesus prayed that a change would come over Him; a change in His energy level, a change in His spiritual power level, a change in His divine enablement level, a change in His love level, a change in His earthly level of God-likeness. You see, He came into the midst of conditions that needed to be changed, so He prayed for changes in Himself so that He could set an example for changes in us. Thus, when down in the depths of despair, with nails having pierced His hands and feet, with pain pulsating through His overcharged veins, and with a crown of thorns on His head, His prayer was not: "Father, please make them stop; Father, I can't take the pain; Father, punish these people who are doing this wrong; Father, strike them all dead for committing these sins against you and me." No, His prayer was, rather, *"Father forgive them; for they know not what they do."* "Forgive my persecutors, forgive my executioners, forgive the scribes and the Pharisees, forgive Pilot and Herod, forgive the Jews and the Gentiles, forgive the whole human race (who, in a sense, are all involved in my murder) because they do not know what they are doing." You see, Jesus came, not to condemn the world, but that the world through Him might be saved—He knew that a change had to take place. Yet, despite all the good that He had done, and that still needed to be done, they crucified Him.

Jesus, while on earth, set the ultimate prayer example; He prayed on good days and He prayed on days that did not seem to be so good. He prayed in the sunshine and He prayed in the storm. He prayed when He was seen and sometimes He would depart to a solitary place and pray. He prayed for Himself but, more often than not, He prayed for people like you and me. You see, He knew that we are all made in the image and likeness of God, and that being so made, there is something divine in all of us. He knew that if He could get, through prayer, to the divine essence in us, that the world through Him would be saved. So, unselfishly, He prayed for us and set the ultimate example; we, however, have not patterned after that example—we have rather just gone off on our own, trying to do things our way.

There are times when we find ourselves faced with obstacles that we pray God will remove; conditions that we pray God will alter; things that we need and pray that God will give us. And we wait patiently, hoping that because we trust in God something miraculous will happen. After waiting awhile, however, we often become impatient and upset, and sometimes even begin to question as we wait for an answer that does not seem to be forthcoming. We wait for God to open doors that have been closed, rather than looking for doors that He has opened. You see, it is easy, because of our human frailty, for us to let things get out of perspective. We feel, sometimes, that if we ask God nicely enough and often enough that He will do anything we want Him to do. And true, if God so ordains, it will be so. But we forget, sometimes, that we are made in the image and likeness of God, and that God works through us to make things happen. More often than not, we pray that things will change, having lost sight of the fact that **prayer changes people** and that, with God's help, **people change things.** In quest of instant action, we often forget about, or negate, or overlook, our own God-likeness. But Jesus did not just pray on the horrid day for conditions or things; He prayed for people (who were made in the image and likeness of God): "Father forgive them . . . I am not concerned about what is happening to me, I am concerned about what is happening to them. Help them to find the divinity that is within themselves so that they can be what you have ordained for them to be."

Prayer changes people—people change things.

According to an old Hindu legend, there was a time when all men were gods. But they so abused their divinity that Brahma, the chief god, decided to take it away from them and hide it where they would never find it. Where to hide it, however, became the big question.

When the lesser gods were called into council to consider the question, they suggested, "We will bury man's divinity deep in the earth."

But Brahma said, "No, that will never do, for man will dig deep down into the earth and find it."

Then they suggested, "We will sink man's divinity in the deepest ocean."

But again Brahma replied, "No, not there, for man will learn to dive into the deepest waters, will search out the ocean bed, and will find it."

Then the lesser gods said, "We will take it to the top of the highest mountain and there will hide it."

But Brahma again replied, "No, for man will eventually climb every high mountain on the earth."

Then the lesser gods gave up and concluded that they did not know where to hide it, for it seemed that there was no place on earth, at the top of the highest mountain or in the deepest sea, that man would not eventually reach.

Brahma then said, "Here is what we will do with man's divinity. We will hide it deep down in man himself, for he will never think to look for it there."

Ever since then, the legend concludes, man has been going up and down the earth, climbing, digging, diving, exploring, and searching for something that is already within himself.

Some two thousand years ago, on a Friday, Jesus found it and shared it with us; but in the movement that came into being in His Name, the divinity of man has been the best kept secret of the ages.

"For God sent not his Son into the world to condemn the world, but that the world through him might be saved." Or to paraphrase; that the world through Him might be changed. **Prayer changes people—people change things.**

Isaiah prophesied some seven hundred years before: *"He was numbered with the transgressors and bore the sins of many and made intercessions for the transgressors."*

Oh to be like Jesus . . .

Let us pray for strength to be able to pray sincerely (when we are hated, when we are abused, when we are treated unjustly, when we are all but crucified), *"Father forgive them; for they know not what they do."*

The Second Word from the Cross

"An Unexpected Invitation"

"And Jesus said unto him, **'Verily I say unto thee, Today shalt thou be with me in paradise.'** "

—Luke 23:43 (KJV)

Three men were to be crucified: two were convicted criminals who were deserving of the death penalty, and the third was Jesus, who was innocent—against whom they could find no real fault. Yes, Jesus was to be crucified.

Crucifixion was the most horrible form of death imaginable. It was without question the cruelest, the most painful, the most inhumane, the most dastardly, the most shameful of all punishments. It was supposed to have been reserved for slaves, for revolutionaries, and for other criminals whose death was meant to be marked with special infamy. Nothing could be thought of that was more unnatural, more degrading, more humiliating, or more revolting than for a living, human being to be suspended in this way. The idea of a crucifixion, it is thought, was suggested by the old practice of nailing up vermin in a kind of revengeful merriment. Even if death came quickly, with the first strokes into the wound, it would still have been an awful death.

More often than not, however, the victim had to linger for many, many days with the burning pain of nails in his hands and feet, with tortured and overcharged veins and, worst of all, intolerable thirst which became greater and greater with the passing of time. It was almost impossible to keep from moving, trying to get whatever relief one could from the many vestiges of pain, but every bit of movement brought about even more excruciating agony. Yet, although everyone knew the "class" of person for whom such punishment had been designed, and were aware of the unusual agony that came with it, they subjected Jesus to it. They crucified Him.

Fortunately, however, we can turn away from this terrible picture and reflect on the supreme message of Luke's Gospel, which is very simply: if you want to know what God is like, take a look at Jesus.

As we look at Him, we can see how by His strength of soul, by His resignation, and by His love He was able to triumph over the shame, over the cruelty, over the humiliation, and over the horror of it all. And we can see how He was able to convert that symbol of wickedness and evil into a symbol of whatever is good and pure and glorious in the world.

His head hung free in crucifixion so that He was not only able to see what was going on around Him, but was also able to speak. And the words He spoke still stand as a window through which we can look into the heart, the mind, and the soul of the man, Jesus. Through them we can see, exhibited to the full, the serenity, the majesty, and the power which had already made Him illustrious.

Jesus had said, "Come unto me, all ye that labor and are heavy laden and I will give you rest." And on the cross, one of the thieves asks for "rest." Jesus had said, "Suffer the little children to come unto me, and forbid them not, for of such is the Kingdom of God." And on the cross, one of the thieves humbled himself, like a little child, and asked Jesus for an entrance into the Kingdom.

One would have thought that amidst this most unusual adversity, Jesus would have been focusing on how to get through and out of this situation. But, rather, He seemed to have easily triumphed over the suffering and the pain by a self-forgetting love: a love that only He could manifest, a love for which nothing was expected nor could be given in return. While fainting beneath the burdens of the cross, He did not seem concerned about his fatigue, His anguish, His despair, or His pain; He seemed more concerned about those around Him—the daughters of Jerusalem and their children, His murderers and a penitent thief on the cross. Yes, even while experiencing what seemed to have been the worst of adversity, with the salvation of the world hanging in the balance dependent on His faith, the faith of one from whom even God seemed to have turned away, with nothing left to clutch for nor cling to—even then and there with that awesome responsibility—He seemed to have had a mind lifted above Himself, calm enough to think about and pray for other people. Although bearing the sins of the world, He did not forget His human ties and was moved to respond to the request of one who had been changed, a convicted thief. "You have admitted that you did wrong, you have confessed your sins, you have given evidence that you believe; today thou shalt be with me in paradise."

The tragic drama has slowly and painfully unfolded and will soon come to an end. So far as we are concerned, the worst is yet to come; the actual death. The physical, the emotional, and the psychological suffering of Jesus has been intense and prolonged. He whose life was one of love will soon die engulfed by a sea of hatred and the bitter, hellish passion that has surged around Him at the cross. In dejection, chagrin, and self-pity we say to ourselves, "It was good that He came, He did a wonderful work but, unfortunately, He will soon be gone forever; this is the end."

But Jesus says from the cross, "this is not the end because I am an Advocate for My Father. Even though you have gone counter to God's Will and have broken His law—you did not trust, you did not obey, you did not believe, you did not love your neighbor, you did not honor your father nor your mother—no matter what you have done or have not done, there is still room for you in paradise. Be you young, or old, rich or poor, in prison or on your death bed, the message is the same; get yourself right with God and . . . thou shalt be with me in paradise."

"For God so loved the world, that he gave his only begotten Son, that whosoever believeth in him should not perish, but have everlasting life. For God sent not his Son into the world to condemn the world; but that the world through him might be saved."

—John 3:16, 17 (KJV)

"And he said unto Jesus, Lord, (I confess . . . I believe) remember me when thou comest into thy kingdom. And Jesus said unto him, Verily I say unto thee, Today shalt thou be with me in paradise."

—Luke 23:42, 43 (KJV)

An unexpected invitation to paradise . . .

The Third Word from the Cross

"Concern . . ."

"When Jesus therefore saw his mother, and the disciples standing by, whom he loved, he saith unto his mother, **Woman, behold thy son!** Then saith he to the disciple, **behold thy mother!**"
—John 19:26, 27 (KJV)

Jesus' first word from the cross was a word of prayer, not for Himself, but for His enemies. His second word was in response to a prayer request, from a former foe; a penitent thief. His third word was a word of direction for two people who had remained close to Him: His mother and His beloved disciple; *"Woman, behold thy son! . . . behold thy mother."* His concern did not seem to have been for Himself at all; His concern was for others.

As we look at Jesus in retrospect, what do we see? As we reflect on His past and project and prepare for the future, what do we see? As we live through the experience of the life, the trial, the crucifixion, and the death of Jesus, what do we see? We see the man, Jesus, in His fullness of being.

Jesus was sent by God and His arrival was announced by God Himself: "This is my beloved Son, in whom I am well pleased; hear ye him." He came on an awesome mission: *"For God sent not his son into the world to condemn the world, but that the world through him might be saved."* While here on Earth, as He interacted with sinful men, His prime concern seemed to have been to aid all people in gaining a more abundant life; because that was

20

why God sent Him. He clothed the naked, He fed the hungry, He healed the sick, He preached good news to the poor, He raised the dead. He did all those things that should have endeared Him to the people, yet they rejected Him, they cursed Him, they buffeted Him, they scourged Him, they adorned Him with a crown of thorns, and then they did the most dastardly thing that anyone could have ever done; they crucified Him. It appeared, at this point, that He had been abandoned by everyone, even God. Yet through this adversity He was able to manifest the most unusual degree of strength. (As we think of the strongest of us under these same circumstances—the brutality, the cruelty, the injustice, the discomfort, the anguish, the pain, the depression, and the shame—we would surely have succumbed and prayed to be taken in death.)

But Jesus, by His strength of soul, was able to triumph over the shame, over the cruelty, and over the horror of it all, and was able to convert that symbol of slavery into something wonderful.

His head hung free, in crucifixion, so that He was able to see both beneath and all around Him; but more than that, He was able to speak. And His utterances stand today as windows through which we can look into the heart, the mind, and the soul of the man Jesus. Through them we can see, exhibited to the fullest, all the qualities that had made Him such a star attraction: His triumph over suffering, His attention to and concern for those around Him, and His exemplification of a self-forgetting love; love for which nothing was expected in return.

When fainting beneath the burden of the cross, He seemed to have ignored His fatigue, His anguish, His dismay, and His pain in order to plan for the daughters of Jerusalem and their children. And when they were nailing Him to the cross, His mind seemed to have been fixed on prayer for His murderers. Yes, even amidst what seemed to have been unbearable discomfort, agony, and pain, with the salvation of the world hanging in the balance de-pendent on His faith, He could not forget His human ties, and could give directions to two whom He truly loved—His mother and His beloved disciple—*"Woman behold thy son! . . . behold thy mother."* Jesus, to be sure, was not held to the cross by nails; He was held to the cross by love!

Although this seems, to us, to be the end, Jesus says to us from the cross, "This is not the end—there are too many believers for this to end now. The tasteless water of Judaism has turned to the sweet wine of Christianity. I must die for you to live. This is a new beginning. You must comfort, care for, and strengthen one another. The trials, the circumstances, the anguish, the pain, the anxiety, and the uncertainty of the past are all behind us; they are the lesser things."

Rise up, O men of God!
Have done with lesser things;
Give heart and mind and soul and strength
To serve the King of Kings.

—William P. Merrill

"Woman, behold thy son! . . . behold thy mother."

22

The Fourth Word from the Cross

"Forsaken . . ."

"And about the ninth hour Jesus cried with a loud voice, saying, Eli, Eli, lama sabach 'thani? that is to say, *My God, my God, why hast thou forsaken me?"*

—Matthew 27:46 (KJV)

These words of Jesus from the cross are words of startling import. Startling because they seem so out of character for Jesus; startling because they seem so out of character for God.

Jesus came to Earth having been sent by God. His arrival on the scene was no surprise because it had been foretold, and God Himself had announced His appearance: "This is my beloved Son in whom I am well pleased."

While He was here on Earth, He walked among sinful men and women. As He interacted with them, His prime concern was clearly that of aiding all humankind in gaining a more abundant life. *"For God sent not his Son into the world to condemn the world, but that the world through him might be saved."* He healed the sick, fed the hungry, preached good news to the poor, and raised the dead. He did all those things that God had ordained for Him to do.

He lived a short life but a full life, a fruitful life, and a blemishless life; an active life, yet a faultless life; an exemplary life and, yes, a perfect life. Yet despite His goodness, despite His perfectness, and despite His God-likeness, He was subjected to the

23

cruelest, the most dastardly, the most shameful of all punishments—crucifixion. What is the most tragic and most shameful fact of it all, though, is that no one could find any fault in Him. Is it any wonder that after such a long, harrowing, undeserved ordeal that Jesus would cry out, with such apparently mind-numbing despair, *"My God, my God, why hast thou forsaken me?"* These unparalleled words seem to be fitting as a climax to His horrible suffering.

The soldiers cruelly mocked Him. They dragged Him through the streets. They scourged and buffeted Him. They arrayed Him with a crown of thorns and they spat on Him. They despoiled Him of His garments and subjected Him to unbearable shame. Yet despite all of this, He suffered in silence. They pierced His hands and feet, yet He endured the cross, seeming to ignore the agony and the pain. The crowd taunted Him—unkind words even came from the convicted criminals who were crucified with Him—yet He never opened His mouth in complaint. No, in response to all that He suffered, not one cry of complaint escaped from His lips. At this moment, however, when the concentrated wrath of Heaven seemed to descend upon Him, He cried with a loud voice, *"My God, my God, why hast thou forsaken me?"* This was, indeed, a cry that should have melted even the hardest heart.

But is it really God's nature to forsake His own? . . . His own Son? Or was Jesus just repeating a psalm of encouragement, as was often done in the Jewish community? Of old, Jehovah never forsook His people. Again and again He was their refuge in times of trouble. When Israel was in bondage, the people cried out to Him and He heard their cries. When they stood helpless at the Red Sea, He was there to deliver them. When the Hebrew boys were in the fiery furnace, the Lord was with them. But at the cross, where a cry went out that was more plaintive, more piercing, and more urgent than any that had ever been heard, there was no response. Here was a situation more alarming than the Red Sea crisis; the enemies here were more relentless, yet there was no deliverance.

Here a fire burned which was hotter than Nebuchadnezzar's furnace, but there was no one at Jesus' side to comfort Him. He seemed, at this point, to have been abandoned by God and in desolation, desperation, and separation He cried out, *"My God, my God, why hast thou forsaken me?"*

The cry of the suffering servant was different because it was out of character. At first He cried, *"Father, forgive them for they know not what they do."* (This was in accord with His compassionate heart.) Later, He responded to a penitent thief, *"Verily I say unto thee, Today shalt thou be with me in Paradise."* (This was in keeping with His grace toward sinners who would repent.) Later still, He spoke to His mother, *"Woman, behold thy son;"* and to His beloved disciple, *"Behold thy mother."* (This, too, was in character with His often evidenced concern and loving kindness.) But the next cry startles and staggers us all. David said, "I have never seen the righteous forsaken . . ." But here at the cross, things are a little different; we see the righteous one being forsaken and we hear His impassioned cry, *"My God, my God, why hast thou forsaken me?"* It was a cry that made the Earth tremble and which reverberated all over the universe.

Forsaken; . . . one of the most tragic words in human speech. What strange feelings are conjured up by the word: a man forsaken by friends, a wife forsaken by her husband, a child forsaken by his parents . . . But a creature forsaken by his Creator; the Son of God forsaken by God . . . That is by far the most frightening; the evil of evils, the ultimate calamity.

As we reflect on the human nature of the man Jesus, however, we can gain comfort as we experience the greatest of all trials; that temporary withdrawal of the consciousness of God's presence. And as we look for deeper meaning in this strange event of Jesus on the cross, we see Him making atonement for the sins of the world; bearing our sins in His own body on the cross. This "forsakenness," this abandonment, this separation that Jesus is experiencing, we deserve—He truly did not. He was so closely identified with the race He came to save, however, that He felt a burden for its sins and cried out as a representative of humanity: *"My God, my God, why hast thou forsaken me?"*

Yes, Jesus was forsaken. He was forsaken so that we might not be forsaken. He was forsaken so that we might be delivered from our sins and from eternal death. He was forsaken so that He could show His love for us, and make known to us His Justice and His pity. He was forsaken so that He might draw our love to Himself, and thus exhibit for us a pattern of patience unto God. He was forsaken, not to show His despair, but in order to exhibit unshakable faith and trust in His Father.

Yes, it was His will to go before us as an example full of grace and wonder; as a suffering Servant who would excite and incite the world.

The words from the dying Jesus reveal the two sides of the cross. In death lies the promise of life, and in life the remembrance of death. Our redemption is in the death and resurrection of Jesus.

"My God, my God, why hast thou forsaken me?"

The Fifth Word from the Cross

"Agony"

"After this, Jesus knowing that all things were now accomplished, that the Scripture might be fulfilled, saith, **I thirst.**"

—John 19:28 (KJV)

"but whosoever drinketh of the water I shall give him shall never thirst; but the water that I shall give him shall be in him a well of water springing up into everlasting life."

—John 4:14 (KJV)

"In the last day, that great day of the feast, Jesus stood and cried, saying, if any man thirst, let him come unto me, and drink. He that believeth on me, as the Scripture hath saith, out of his belly shall flow rivers of living water."

—John 7:37, 38 (KJV)

Throughout all of the Earthly ministry of Jesus, as He moved from village to hamlet, from mountain to valley, from desert place to seaside and from house to house, preaching, teaching, healing, and generally doing the will of His Father in the midst of the people, His primary concern seemed always to have been that of aiding humankind in gaining a more abundant life. He never seemed concerned about Himself; it was always for the healing of the sick, or the uplifting of the fallen, or the feeding of the hungry, or the giving of hope to the hopeless, or the alleviating of oppression—in a word, for providing something special for somebody else. And here, on the cross, even after having endured the humiliation, the anguish, the agony, the pain, and the suffering leading up to His crucifixion, His focus still seemed to be the same; He still evidenced a concern for others.

In His first two utterances from the cross, He showed compassionate concern for those who had humiliated and tortured Him—His persecutors—and for a thief who had repented: *"Father forgive them; for they know not what they do,"* and *"Today thou shalt be with me in paradise."* Again, in the next, with seemingly no regard for Himself or His situation, His concern was for the welfare of His mother and His beloved Disciple: *"Woman, behold thy son!"* And then, to the disciple, *"Behold thy mother!"* In the fourth word, when He cried, *"My God, my God, why hast thou forsaken me?,"* it was not a cry of despair. No! It was, rather, more evidence of His unshakable faith and trust in His Heavenly Father. He was letting those around Him know that He was forsaken so that we would not be forsaken; He was forsaken so that we could be saved. The first four utterances, it is very clear, were made with the well-being of others in mind.

In this fifth word, however, Jesus says, *"I thirst."* (**I** . . . thirst.) This utterance is very different from all the rest because in it, for the first time, He is calling attention to Himself. Here, for the first time, He seems to be revealing something personal about Himself; something special, something like nothing we have ever heard before. These words were not merely spoken, so *"that the scripture might be fulfilled,"* as the casual reader might assume, nor were they spoken because Jesus was seeking out or looking for pity. No! It seems obvious that Jesus was feeling something that He wanted the people to know about. What was being revealed, although most of the people didn't understand it, was something that was far more than just a physical desire; it was more than that.

To be sure, there was a physical thirst. The road had been rough. The treatment of Jesus had been unusually brutal and cruel. The physical suffering had been intense and prolonged. After having fainted under the weight of the cross, he had been forced to hang on it for three days in the noonday sun and two nights in darkness. His head ached, His eyes were running, His mouth was parched, and His throat was burning. He had to endure the burning pain of nails in His hands and feet, the torture of overcharged veins, the crown of thorns on His head and, worst of all, His intolerable thirst which became greater and greater with the passing of time. (They offered Him vinegar mixed with gall, a drink that the soldiers used to deaden pain, but He would not accept it. He wanted to be in complete control of His faculties throughout this sordid experience.) Hunger is painful, and often difficult, but it is nothing as compared to thirst.

The time, the torture, the pain, the anxiety, the dust, the heat, and the separation had all taken their toll on the mind and on the weak and weary body of Jesus. Now, however, after having struggled to shoulder a cross in the heat of the day, with the heavy loss of blood from the scourging and the crown of thorns, with the pulsating of His overcharged veins, the burning in His throat and with his lips, parched, dry, cracked and bleeding, Jesus did not make a request; rather, He revealed His condition—"*I thirst.*"

Knowing the character of Jesus, He could not have been concerned only about his physical condition. What was He saying? Was He, perhaps, trying to tell the people that there was no more that He could do for them? Was He trying to tell them that all He once had was now gone; that it had been taken away? Was He, like a spent athlete, collapsing after the completion of a grueling test of strength and will, and yielding to others for refreshment and sustenance? Was He throwing in the towel? What more could there have been in that utterance: "*I thirst?*"

His thirst was, indeed, a physical thirst but, it was much more than that. By saying "*I thirst,*" Jesus was identifying Himself as the Savior promised in scripture. In the scripture it had been written that the Messiah would be a suffering Messiah. So, in this utterance, Jesus was identifying Himself as the One who fulfills the scriptural picture of the Deliverer who is to come.

His thirst on the cross was a public showing forth of His humility, of His dependence, of His oneness with God. (Even though He was human, He was still connected with God.) His thirst was a thirst after righteousness. His thirst was for the salvation of the sin-sick soul. His thirst was for abundant life for "the least of these," for you and me. His thirst was for the atonement of our sins, and for the sins of the whole world.

> "For God so loved the world, that he gave his only begotten Son, that whosoever believeth in him should not perish, but have everlasting life. For God sent not his Son into the world to condemn the world; but that the world through him might be saved."
> —John 3:16, 17 (KJV)

His thirst was for physical refreshment. His thirst was for our salvation. His thirst was for our eternal life. His thirst was for strength to voluntarily commit Himself to death.

> "After this, Jesus knowing that all things were now accomplished, that the Scripture might be fulfilled, saith, **I thirst**."

The Sixth Word from the Cross

"Triumph"

"When Jesus therefore had received the vinegar, he said, **it is finished:** and bowed his head and gave up the ghost."

—John 19:30 (KJV)

The first three utterances from Jesus on the cross **called attention to His compassion and concern for others:** He prayed for those who had brutally persecuted Him, He responded positively to the request of a penitent thief, and He made provisions for both His mother and His beloved disciple. The fourth word **called attention to what had happened to Him, in our behalf:** He was forsaken that we would not be forsaken; forsaken so that we would be saved. The fifth word **called attention to Himself; Jesus, the person—"I thirst."** (Here, Jesus was not making a request but was, rather, making a statement about His condition.) The sixth word **called attention to His work** of the cross—the task that had been assigned to His hands, the goal that He had set out to reach—*"It is finished."*

Many of those who had been in the company of Jesus had no idea why He had come nor what He had come to do. All were amazed by the unusual way that He was able to just make things happen, but why He had come, they could not seem to figure out. Jesus' focus, however, was very clear. He knew that God had sent Him on a great mission and, no matter how magnanimous the task might have appeared, Jesus knew that only He could accomplish it.

One has cause to wonder about the sixth utterance: was it a sigh of relief or a shout of exaltation? a cry out of sadness or a statement of joy? a suggestion of fulfillment or a murmur of disappointment? a word of defeat or an exclamation of victory? a message to His Father or a proclamation to men? Had Jesus been able to reach His goal—to complete the exalted task assigned to His hand, to the satisfaction of His Father—or had He failed miserably? What was the meaning of that utterance?

Jesus came into a world that was wrought with discord, confusion, turmoil, evil, wickedness, hate—a world of sin. He came, however, not to condemn the world, but that the world through Him might be saved. But the works of His hands, although ordained by God and for the greater good, were cause for much suffering, humiliation, and shame. He was dragged through the streets, cruelly mocked, scourged, buffeted, arrayed with a crown of thorns, spat on, not because of doing what was wrong but because of doing what was right and good. He was despoiled of His clothes and was subjected to unbearable pain and shame, yet He suffered in silence. He was forced to carry a wooden cross, to which His hands and feet were later nailed, yet He endured the cross, seeming to ignore the agony and the pain. He was taunted by the crowd—unkind words even came from the criminals who were being crucified with Him—yet He never opened His mouth in complaint.

But gladly we can turn away from the horrible pictures we have just seen, and the awful thoughts that we now have, and can reflect on the supreme message that comes forth with real force, which is very simply: if you want to know what God is like, take a look at Jesus.

As we look at Him, we can see how, by His strength of soul, by His resignation, and by His love, He was able to triumph over the shame, the humiliation and the horror of it all. We see, too, how He was able to convert that symbol of slavery and wickedness into a symbol of whatever is most pure and glorious in the world.

The tragic drama has slowly and painfully unfolded and is soon to come to an end. As far as we are concerned, the worst is yet to come; the actual death. The physical suffering of Jesus was prolonged. He whose very life was one of love will soon die engulfed by a sea of hatred and the bitter, hellish passion that has surged around Him at the cross. And in dejection, chagrin, and self-pity, we say to ourselves, "It was good that He came—He did many wonderful things—but unfortunately, He will be gone forever; this is the end."

But Jesus says from the cross, "This is not the end for Me; this is just the end of this phase. *It is finished.*" Jesus, at the age of twelve, said that He had to be about His Father's business. Now twenty-one years later, while dying on the cross, He says, *"It is finished!"*

In the Greek, the word *tetelestai* is used and is interpreted as *finished.* It is a word that was very familiar in everyday usage. Farmers used it when a new and flawless animal was born. Servants used it when they had completed tasks that had been assigned to them. Artists used it after they had completed a masterpiece. Priests used it after having examined sacrifices at the altar of God; if they were deemed perfect, flawless, and suitable for presentation unto God, they would say *tetelestai.* Jesus used it to indicate that He had completed the picture begun in the Old Testament.

We should, therefore, not be concerned about how the story seems (to us) to end; Jesus did what He was sent here to do. He was a living example. . . . He was a faithful Savior. His work was perfect. His life and work were complete. His death, though apparently put in motion by men, was in the Divine plan of God. Jesus gave His life for us.

Tetelestai, tetelestai—it is perfect, it is flawless, it is complete—*"It is finished."*

The Seventh Word from the Cross

"Submission"

"And when Jesus had cried with a loud voice, he said, Father into thy hands I commend my spirit: and having said thus, he gave up the ghost."

—Luke 23:46 (KJV)

The shadow fell, the sun's light failed, there was darkness all over the land, and the curtain of the temple was torn in two. . . The tormentors had become weary and most had left. The tumult and the shouting had died down. Then Jesus, crying in a loud voice, said, *". . . Father into thy hands I commend my spirit: and having said thus, he gave up the ghost."*

These words not only tell how Jesus died, but they also tell how Jesus lived.

Through His earthly life and ministry, Jesus leaned heavily on the word of God for all that He did and all that He said. His life and His actions had clearly been planned out by God, and His actions made us know that He was following the blueprint that God had set forth. He used the scriptures or referred to them in His daily discourses, in His preaching, and in His teaching. *"It is written . . ."* He would often say, or *". . . you have read . . ."* or *"How readest thou?"* He was so accustomed to using the scriptures that it does not seem strange at all that He would quote from the thirty-first Psalm at this awful hour, *"Into thine hands I commit my spirit."* But the intent of the words, in these two instances, was quite different. The cry of the Psalmist was that of a sinner fleeing to God for salvation. The Savior's words, on the other hand, were those of a victor going to God with salvation—salvation won by His own hand.

Jesus lived a short life, but He lived a full life: a good life, a fruitful life, a blemishless life, an exemplary life, a productive life, a perfect life. Yet despite His goodness, despite His perfectness, despite His God-likeness, He was subjected to the cruelest, the most shameful, the most dastardly of all punishments—crucifixion. He was hated by those whom His perfect life condemned. And the most tragic and shameful fact of it all is that no one could find any fault with Him.

The soldiers mocked Him, they dragged Him through the streets, they scourged Him, they buffeted Him, they arrayed Him with a crown of thorns; they even spat on Him. They despoiled Him of His clothes and subjected Him to unbearable humiliation, agony, and shame, yet He suffered in silence. They pierced His hands and feet, yet He endured the cross, seeming to ignore the agony and the pain. His friends forsook Him, the crowd taunted Him—unkind words came even from the convicted criminals who were to be crucified with Him—yet He never opened His mouth in complaint. No, in response to all that He suffered at the hands of those sinful men, not one complaint escaped from His mouth.

But as we reflect here on the human nature of the man Jesus, we can gain comfort as we experience, with Him, the greatest of all trials; that temporary withdrawal of the consciousness of God's presence. And as we look for deeper meaning in this strange experience of Jesus on the cross, we see Him making atonement for the sins of the whole world (for us); bearing our sins in His body on the cross. He was so closely identified with the race He came to save, that He felt the burdens of our sins and cried out as a representative of all humanity. He was forsaken that we might not be forsaken but, rather, be delivered from our sins and from eternal death. Yes, He chose to go before us as an example full of wonder;

as a suffering servant who would excite and incite the world, and turn it upside down.

Is it any wonder, after all He had done for us, during the many hours of torture, discomfort, heartache, and pain, that He would finally utter a word that would call attention to Himself—not a request, just a word? *"I thirst."*

As the ordeal of those last days came to an end, Jesus said, **"It is finished.** Father, I did what you sent me to do; You didn't want the world condemned, you wanted it saved. The appointed work is finished, the job is complete, it is perfect; there is nothing more for me to do. I don't have to let myself be tortured anymore. I don't have to suffer any more shame. There is no need in letting myself be subjected to the whims of merciless, senseless, wicked, sinful men anymore. I'm ready to leave the unkind treatment of the human race. I've set the example that You directed me to set. I'm ready now to give up this earthly life. I have used it to Your honor and glory; now, I commend it to You."

"And when Jesus had cried with a loud voice, he said, Father, into thy hands I commend my spirit; and having said thus, he gave up the ghost."

The death of Jesus was different. It was a *victorious death;* that is, He took His spoils with Him. It was a *vicarious death*; that is, no man took His life—He commended it to God, from Whom it had come. His life, under His direction, became united again with the life of God.

Our slave forefathers, understanding the example that Jesus set, sang: "Soon I will be done with the troubles of this world, goin' home to live with God." But the words of the Psalmist and of the Spiritual writer were words of sinners seeking salvation. The words of Jesus, on that fateful day, however, were words of a victor going to God with salvation—salvation that He had won, for us, by His own doing.

Jesus Christ became obedient for us unto death; even the death of the cross.

"Father, into Thy hands I commend My spirit . . ."

Prayer

Jesus, keep me near the cross;
There a precious fountain
Free to all a healing stream,
Flows from Calvary's mountain.

—Fanny J. Crosby

Easter Morning

"And the angel answered and said unto the women, Fear not ye: for I know that ye seek Jesus which was crucified. He is not here: for he is risen, as he said. Come, see the place where the Lord lay."
—Matthew 28:5, 6 (KJV)

Jesus died in His own way; the way that it had been ordained for Him to die. His death was in complete submission to the Will of God. God had used His Son to the honor and glory of God, and God was with Him until the end. After Jesus died, He lay in a tomb; a tomb which, it was thought, had been sealed forever. This, everyone thought, was the end of Jesus.

When the Sabbath was over, and it was almost daybreak. Mary Magdalene and the other Mary went to see the tomb where Jesus lay. Prior to their arrival, however, a strong earthquake struck, and an angel of the Lord came down from heaven, rolled the stone away, and sat on it. The angel looked as bright as lightning, and his clothes were as white as snow. Those who had been assigned to guard the tomb had been so overcome with fear that they had fallen down as though they were dead.

The angel said to the women, "Don't be afraid! I know you came looking for Jesus who was crucified on the cross and died. God has raised him from the dead, just as He said He would. You are looking for the living among the dead. Jesus lives!"

A Lesson Learned

"Know ye not, that so many of us as were baptized into Jesus Christ were baptized into death? Therefore we are buried with him by baptism into death: that like as Christ was raised up from the dead by the glory of the Father, even so we also should walk in newness of life. For if we have been planted together in the likeness of his death, we shall be also in the likeness of his resurrection: knowing this, that our old man is crucified with him, that the body of sin might be destroyed, that henceforth we should not serve sin. For he that is dead is free from sin. Now if we be dead with Christ, we believe that we shall also live with him: knowing that Christ being raised from the dead dieth no more; death has no more dominion over him. For in that he died, he died unto sin once: but in that he liveth, he liveth unto God. Likewise reckon ye also yourselves to be dead indeed unto sin, but alive unto God through Jesus Christ our Lord."

—Romans 6:3–11 (KJV)

On the Cross

WHILE ON THE CROSS
He set an example . . .
HE MADE THE FACT KNOWN
He was about His Father's business.
HIS MISSION WAS CLEAR
He was to weld the condition of brokenness
between God and humanity.
EVEN AMIDST ADVERSITY
He continued in pursuit of His mission.
HE EXHIBITED LOVE
The kind of love for which nothing
was expected in return.
HE TAUGHT US TO LIVE
fearlessly yet passionately.
HE WAS HUMBLE
in His submission to His Father.
HE DIED
that we might live.
HE AROSE
that we might have newness of life.
HIS STORY WAS
one of suffering to death, of resurrection to life.

Amen